Managing Your Intellectual Property Assets

Managing Your Intellectual Property Assets

Scott Shane

First published in 2008 by
Business Expert Press, LLC
222 East 46th Street, New York, NY 10017
www.businessexpertpress.com

ISBN-13: 978-1-60649-027-3 (paperback)
ISBN-10: 1-60649-027-3 (paperback)

ISBN-13: 978-1-60649-028-0 (e-book)
ISBN-10: 1-60649-028-1 (e-book)

DOI 10.4128/9781606490280

A publication in the Entrepreneurship and Small Business Management collection

Collection ISSN (print) 1946-5653
Collection ISSN (electronic) 1946-5661

Cover design by Artistic Group—Monroe, NY
Interior design by Scribe, Inc.

First edition: November 2008

10 9 8 7 6 5 4 3 2 1

Printed in the United States of America.

Abstract

We now live in a world in which intellectual property is very important, accounting for a large portion of the value provided by many companies. Unfortunately most managers and entrepreneurs do not understand how to manage their companies' intellectual property. This book looks at why patents, trade secrets, trademarks, and copyrights are important; what they do; and how to use them to generate competitive advantage and profit for your company.

Keywords

Copyrights, intellectual property, patents, trademarks, trade secrets

Contents

Introduction

Intellectual property is of great importance to many companies. In fact, at some public companies, intellectual property now accounts for as much as 70% of the value of business.[1] Because intellectual property is an important source of value in companies in high-technology industries, managing intellectual property is an important part of technology strategy.

As a technology entrepreneur or manager, you need to understand the different legal mechanisms that you can use to protect your intellectual property, and you need to develop ways to employ those mechanisms to your advantage. This book focuses on the four ways that companies protect their intellectual property through legal means: patents, trade secrets, copyrights, and trademarks.

The first section discusses why companies need intellectual property protection. The second section identifies what is patentable. The third and fourth sections identify the parts of a patent and describe how to use a patent, respectively. The fifth section helps you to decide whether or not you should patent your inventions. The sixth, seventh, and eighth sections discuss secrecy, copyrights, and trademarks respectively.

Why You Need Intellectual Property Protection

Before you can understand how to use patents, trade secrets, copyrights, and trademarks as strategic tools, you first need to understand why you need intellectual property protection at all. The answer lies in the components of a successful technology strategy. Introducing an innovative new product or service that meets the needs of customers is a necessary but not sufficient condition for success. Success also depends on protecting your product or service, or the way it is produced and sold, against imitation by competitors. Otherwise, your competitors rather than you will capture the profits that flow from your innovation.

Why is the ability of competitors to imitate your products and services so problematic to your profitability as an innovator? The answer is simple. You need to earn a profit on the sale of those innovative products and services to recoup the investment that you made to develop them. Initially, when you introduce a new product or service, you will have a monopoly; no one else yet offers a product or service that meets the same needs of the market you are serving. Your monopoly position allows you to charge high enough prices to generate the profit margins that you need to recoup your investment.

Unfortunately, any success that you have will motivate your competitors to copy what you are doing. If your competitors can come up with a product or service that meets the same customer need, or they can undermine your advantages in producing or selling your product by copying how you do those things, then they can capture some of the profits that you are earning. To make matters worse, the more successful you are at the introduction of the new product or service—and the less you want to be imitated—the more motivated your competitors will be to imitate what you are doing. Your success makes it more obvious that competitors *should* imitate you—and in many cases it provides them with the information that they need to imitate your new product or service, or your method of producing and selling it, successfully.

If imitators are not stopped, they will undermine all of your profit. To produce their copies of your initial product or service, imitators need to get access to the same resources that you are using: the employees, the capital, and the raw materials. As a result, they bid up the prices of these resources, causing your profit margins to fall. Moreover, the imitators take away some of your customers. Each customer that they woo away from you drives down your revenues, further hurting your profit margins.

Clearly, you need to stop your competitors from imitating your new products or services if you are going to be successful. Unfortunately, doing this is not easy. Most new products are simple to copy, particularly for large, established firms. One study by Richard Levin and his colleagues showed that approximately half of the time, the average unpatented new product can be duplicated by 6–10 competitors, at less than half the cost of the original development.[1] Edwin Mansfield performed another study, which showed that, on average, one third of new products can be imitated in 6 months or less.[2]

Companies can figure out how to imitate your new products and services in a wide variety of ways. Many new products can be reverse engineered, with your competitor's technical staff simply taking apart your new product and figuring out how it works. Once their engineers figure out how your product works, it is often very easy for them to come up with another way to do exactly the same thing.[3]

Your competitors can easily hire your employees as a way to learn what they know. Labor markets are free in most countries, and people often leave their jobs to go work for competitors. So your competitors could figure out how to imitate your products and services by offering a higher salary to your employees to get them to jump ship. Then they can use the knowledge that your employees have developed while working for your company to create products and services that imitate yours.

Sometimes simply working on similar new products allows your competitors to figure out how to copy your new products or services. Most companies are working on new products and services that are similar to each other, and just knowing that your company has figured out a way to, say, make a product smaller or add features to it, is sometimes enough to allow your competitors to come up with an imitative product or service on their own.[4]

Your competitors can also look at public documents and publications to figure out how to copy your new product or service.[5] Because engineers and scientists have strong expertise in the area in which they work, they can often extrapolate from partial information obtained in public sources and figure out how to imitate your new products or services, just on the basis of information that you have made public.

What Is Patentable?

A patent is a government-granted monopoly that precludes others from using an invention for 20 years (for utility patents) in return for the inventor's disclosure about how the invention operates. Patents are based on a fundamental trade-off. As compensation for showing others how an invention works, and thereby advancing the level of technical knowledge in a country, inventors receive monopoly rights to their invention for a specific period of time.

Patents have a complex set of effects on technological innovation. On the one hand, they provide people with an incentive to innovate. In the absence of the monopoly right provided by patents, inventors often would be unable to capture the value coming from their inventions and, therefore, be unwilling to develop or exploit them. Moreover, the disclosure that patents require makes it possible for other parties to learn from inventions and make further advances, which would not be possible if the inventors kept the inventions secret.

On the other hand, patents can deter technological innovation by making it difficult for others to reap commercial value from undertaking further developments in an area, given the inventor's property rights. For example, some observers believe that patents on genes deter follow-on innovation because they give the patent holder too much protection, thus deterring others from developing genetic tests based on the initial inventor's discovery.

Patenting is an old, and established, form of intellectual property protection. The first uses of patents go back centuries; patents were important mechanisms to protect basic inventions of the industrial revolution, such as the steam engine. The patent system is so important that in the United States the patent system is enshrined in Article I of the Constitution, and has existed since the birth of the nation.

Despite being around a long time, patenting appears to be increasing in importance. Since 1983, the number of patents granted by the U.S. Patent and Trademark Office (USPTO) has increased by approximately

5.7% annually.[1] Currently, each year approximately 350,000 patent applications are made to the USPTO, 200,000 patents are awarded, and inventors spend in excess of $5 billion to obtain U.S. patents to protect their inventions.[2]

What Can Be Patented?

Many brilliant business concepts cannot be protected with patents because only the mechanisms for exploiting ideas can be patented, not the ideas themselves.[3] For example, you cannot patent the idea of a fast-food restaurant drive-through window. All you can do is patent a mechanism for exploiting the idea, such as the window itself.

Because they are not embodied in physical form, most services are difficult to patent.[4] So you cannot patent courteous service, even if it provides your business with a competitive edge. The best that you can do is to patent the process by which that service is created, as would be the case if you developed a robotic employee that could be programmed to be courteous all of the time, even if it were having a bad day.

You also cannot patent laws of nature or any substances that appear naturally,[5] such as chemical elements, because the government thinks of nature, not the person discovering them, as the inventor. The best that you can do to protect a discovery of a natural substance is to patent the mechanisms for obtaining it, such as the process of leaching iron from rock.[6]

You can get a utility patent, which is given for new or improved products and processes, for one of four things: a process (such as a chemical reaction), a machine (such as a laser), an article of manufacture (such as a diskette), or a composition of matter (such as a genetically altered bacterium).[7]

Novel, Nonobvious, and Useful

Patents are only granted for inventions that the patent office determines are novel, nonobvious, and useful. The USPTO defines an invention as "novel" if it has not been previously invented.[8]

The patent office deems an invention to be "obvious" if it is a clear next step in technological development to a person of ordinary skill in the field of the purported invention (for example, an electrical engineer would be considered to have ordinary skill and knowledge with respect to electrical circuits) or if the elements of the invention all were present in existing patents and it would be obvious to combine those elements.[9] For example, J. M. Smucker Co. was denied a patent on its method of applying filling to its "Uncrustables" sandwich product because the patent examiner assigned to the case believed that the concept of applying peanut butter on one slice of bread and applying jelly on another would be "obvious" to anyone trained in the art of making a sandwich.[10]

For the USPTO to view an invention as "useful," it has to work, have a use, and be functional.[11] So you cannot patent something that is not functional, such as a piece of music. However, being "useful" does not mean that an invention has to have commercial value; in fact, most patented inventions generate no financial returns. Take, for example, U.S. patent 5,023,850, for a dog watch that moves at 7 times the rate of a normal watch.[12] While this device works, is functional, and has a purpose, it has no commercial value. Perhaps the number of dogs who can tell time and have disposable income is too small.

First to Invent

The U.S. patent system differs from the patent systems in most other countries because the United States awards patents to the first party to invent something, not to the first inventor to file for a patent. The importance of the first-to-invent rule can be seen in the case of the rotational wheel interface in Apple Computer Inc.'s iPod. Microsoft was the first company to file for a patent on this technology, which is currently the subject of a patent dispute between Apple and Microsoft. For Apple to prevail in this dispute, it has to file a declaration to the U.S. Patent and Trademark Office (USPTO), which states that it invented the device before Microsoft, and the USPTO has to determine, as a result of an investigation of the declaration and Apple's records, that Apple's invention predated Microsoft's patent application.[13]

Nondisclosure

In the United States, patents are only awarded for inventions that have not been offered for sale and have not been publicly disclosed, either in an open forum or in print, more than one year earlier.[14] While experimental testing of your invention is not considered public use, you cannot advertise the invention, issue a press release about it, present it in a seminar, or even offer a description of it at a trade show.[15] In fact, in some cases, even showing an invention to your friends might constitute a public disclosure of the invention. So, to keep your invention secret, you need to have anyone who looks at the invention before you file for a patent sign a nondisclosure agreement.[16]

Expansion of What Is Patentable

Over time, the U.S. government has steadily expanded the types of things that can be protected by a patent, leading to a rise in the number of patents issued. Since 1980, patents can be obtained on genetically engineered organisms, such as mice; genetically altered substances, such as yeast; and human genetic sequences.[17]

In addition, while mathematical formulas are considered to be natural phenomena and cannot be patented,[18] those formulas that are applied to a structure or process (as occurs in software) have been patentable since 1981.[19] As a result, patents now protect a wide range of computer software—from training tools to investment and insurance systems to e-commerce payment mechanisms.[20] Furthermore, since 1998, business methods can be protected by patents.[21]

The expansion of what is patentable has raised a number of important issues for technology strategy:

1. The increase in the volume of patent applications has created backlogs in the patent office, making the process of getting a patent less efficient than it used to be.
2. The growth in the patent "thicket" has resulted in a lot of cumulative and overlapping patents, increasing the rate at which firms license their patents to each other (cross-licensing).

3. The expansion into business method patents, which tend to be broader and more obvious than other patents, has raised questions about the degree to which innovation is being hindered by property rights.

4. The expansion into genetically engineered organisms has raised questions about whether they block follow-on research and are making it difficult to come up with new medical and pharmaceutical innovations.

Design and Plant Patents

There are two types of patents other than utility patents, which we have been discussing: design patents and plant patents. Design patents are given for the appearance of products.[22] For example, U.S. patent number D339456 protects an ornamental design for a shoe sole. Design patents differ from utility patents because they have only one claim and protect a piece of intellectual property for only 14 years.[23]

Plant patents are given only for engineered plants that are reproduced asexually.[24] An example is Tropicana's patent for varieties of oranges used in its Pure Premium orange juice. Like utility patents, plant patents protect a piece of intellectual property for 20 years and have multiple claims.

The Parts of a Patent

Patents have two key parts: the specification and the claims. The specification is a description of how the invention works and may include accompanying illustrations. The specification is what you must trade off in return for the monopoly right that you receive. Its purpose is to allow those skilled in the relevant technical area to reproduce your invention.[1]

The other major part of a patent is the set of claims, or the statements that identify a particular feature or combination of features that are protected by the patent. The claims are what indicate whether another patent infringes your patent—that is, violates your monopoly right. As an inventor, you want to obtain a patent with broad scope claims (as long as you can enforce them) because a patent prevents imitation of only those things specified in the claims. The broader the scope of the claims, the harder it is for other firms to make changes to your invention and work around your claims. For example, Jet Dock Systems Inc. has a patent for floating dry docks, made of connected plastic cubes. But instead of having a patent that covers just the cubes or their method of assembly, Jet Dock Systems Inc. has a patent on the process of drive-on docking. As a result, the company's patent bars competitors that use a different method of assembly of a floating dry dock from imitating its product.[2]

While broad scope claims are valuable for the reasons just described, you also need to ensure that your patent will be held as valid if challenged and that you will be able to prove infringement. The broader the scope of your claims and the better it protects your innovation, the more likely other people will be to challenge it, in the hopes that they can get rid of your monopoly right and do what you are doing.

Unfortunately for the patent holder, patents with very broad claims are often difficult to enforce. The less specific the claims, the less easily judges and juries can interpret the words in them.[3] In addition, patents with very broad claims that cover entire methods of approaching problems, rather than just specific products, are more likely to be deemed invalid. For example, a federal appeals court recently invalidated a

University of Rochester patent on Cox-2 inhibitors, saying that the patent's claims were too general for the patent to be valid. This caused the University of Rochester to lose its lawsuit against Pfizer Inc. for infringement of the university's patent by its drug Celebrex.

So how do you know how strong your patent's claims are? You need to look at the patent to see if part of the claims could be changed or dropped and still yield the same level of protection. For example, if a patent claims the process for using a particular adhesive for attaching two pieces of metal, but you could easily attach the two pieces of metal with another adhesive, then the patent has weak claims. All that a competitor has to do to get around your adhesive patent is to substitute a different adhesive for the one that you have claimed.

Sometimes companies cannot get one or two broad claims and, therefore, try to protect their inventions with a large number of claims. Sometimes the number of claims that inventors make on their patents are quite large, numbering in the hundreds.

Pioneering patents—basic patents in a technical area on which a wide range of patents can be built—are a special case of patents with strong claims. Control of these patents is important because they can be used to extract royalty payments from a large number of users. For example, the holders of pioneering patents in genetic engineering earned hundreds of millions of dollars in royalties from a variety of companies using genetic engineering techniques to make drugs. Similarly, NEC Corp. has made a great deal of money licensing its pioneering patents on carbon nanotubes, which are being used for fuel-cell batteries in notebook computers, transistors, wide-screen televisions, and sensors.[4]

Pioneering patents and patents with broad claims are especially important to you if you are starting a company. New firms often lack other forms of competitive advantage when they are first established. Strong patents allow you to create the value chain for your new business and establish additional competitive advantages before your new product or service is imitated by other firms.

The more pioneering your patent and the broader its scope, the more competitor firms you can deter from imitating your new product or service. For example, Friendster recently obtained a patent on the method of searching for people on the Web as a function of their social ties. Because this patent is so broad, Friendster can use it to stop Facebook and MyS-pace from engaging in similar Web-based social networking activities, or at least to obtain licensing fees from them if they do. Consequently, the patent will help the start-up, whose performance has lagged as a result of competition from these two companies.[5]

Defining the Claims

The claims that you are allowed to make are limited by what previous inventors, whose patents have already been granted, have claimed. The initial arbiter of what claims you can get is the patent examiner. To help patent examiners determine what claims should be granted, as an inventor, you have a duty to provide citations to previous patents whose technical art you built upon in creating your inventions. These citations limit your property right to only those things not claimed in previously cited patents.

To disallow a claim, patent examiners must provide legal reasons for their actions. If an examiner denies a claim file, an inventor can file a response to the examiner and have that response evaluated. If the decisions remain negative after this revision, then an inventor can appeal to the Board of Patent Appeals for a conference with senior patent examiners. This appeal can result in either a reversal of the examiner or a continued rejection of the patent application. If an inventor fails to obtain positive decisions at the level of the Board of Patent Appeals, he or she can ask the Board of Examiners to consider the issue.[6]

Although patent examiners are very good at determining what claims should be granted, they sometimes grant patents that are too broad or that overlap. For example, many observers have criticized the U.S. Patent and Trademark Office (USPTO) for initially allowing very broad claims on genetic engineering and Internet business method patents.[7] These broad claims may have increased the cost of developing new products by creating conflicting claims.

It is important to note how human the patenting process is. Patents are not an objective exclusion device created by machines. Rather, they are the result of interpretations by human beings and a complex negotiating process. As a result, some issued patents make sense and others do not. Moreover, sometimes inventors who deserve patents are denied them.

Who Can Apply?

Only inventors can apply for and be awarded patents. If you employ or contract for work done by others and would like to own the patents on any resulting inventions, you need your employees or contractors to agree in writing to assign those patents to you. Otherwise, U.S. law assumes that employees and independent contractors own the rights to the inventions that they make. To facilitate this assignment process, many companies specify this assignment in their employment agreements.[8]

The limitation on who can be awarded a patent raises an important issue for start-up firms. Inventors who found companies based on their inventions own the patents awarded for those inventions unless they assign them to their companies. To protect themselves, investors in start-up companies typically require inventor-founders to assign those patents to their companies. That way, if the venture does not do well, the investors have access to the business's intellectual property assets and can sell them to recoup some of their losses. Of course, this means that inventors may lose control of their own inventions if their start-ups, which use these inventions, are unsuccessful.

Using a Patent

As a technology strategist, you also need to understand how to use patents effectively. This chapter discusses two important issues: the use of multiple patents to protect technology and the use of the legal system to enforce patents.

Picket Fences and Brackets

Although you might try to obtain a broad patent with strong claims to protect your invention, such patents are not always possible. As a result, you might want to apply for more than one patent to protect your new product or service. For example, if you run a biotechnology company that has invented a new drug, you might try to patent both the molecule itself and the process for producing it.

If you cannot get a single broad patent to protect your invention, then building a picket fence of patents around the core invention can be a way to protect your new product or service. For example, when Gillette developed the Sensor razor, it obtained 22 different patents to protect the product, including patents on the blades, the handle design, and the packaging container.[1] Because your competitors' ability to imitate your invention without infringing on your patents depends on coming up with a way to do the same thing as your invention in a way not indicated in your patent claims, then obtaining a variety of patents can deter imitation by closing off alternative paths.

Because companies build picket fences of packet protection around their inventions, other companies engage in bracketing—the process of keeping an inventor from using his or her invention by patenting around it—to counteract their efforts. For example, if your competitor has obtained a patent on a filament for a new, higher intensity light, you can keep your competitor from using its filament patent by patenting ancillary inventions, such as a new bulb, new housing, new connections, and a new shade, thereby bracketing the filament patent with your own patents on the rest of the light.[2]

Patent Litigation

Because patents only provide you with the right to sue to collect damages from others who infringe your patents, successful strategies for exploiting patents invariably involve legal action. Therefore, intellectual property litigation is, and has always been, an integral part of technology strategy.

But before we can discuss how you can enforce your patents, you first have to know what patent infringement is. Infringement occurs when someone to whom you have not licensed your invention makes, uses, sells, or imports something covered by the claims of your patent. Your invention does not have to be duplicated in its entirety for your invention to be infringed. If any part of what is claimed is duplicated, infringement has occurred. Moreover, infringement can occur inadvertently as well as deliberately and can occur if one party induces another to build something that is covered by your patent.[3]

So how do you know if your patent has been infringed? Infringement occurs if another invention does substantially the same thing, in the same way, with the same result, as a patented invention. For example, a new bicycle wheel would infringe an existing bicycle wheel patent even if the second bicycle wheel was not exactly the same as the first but performed the same function in a similar manner to the patented wheel.[4] But a patent on the engine of a fuel-cell powered car would not infringe a patent on a car powered by an internal combustion engine. Even though the two technologies both make the car go, the two kinds of engines do so in very different ways: one by turning hydrogen into water and the other by burning gasoline.

If you suspect that your patent has been infringed, then you should take legal action immediately. If you wait too long to enforce your patent rights, then the courts will presume that you know about the infringement and do not care to take action.[5] After filing a patent infringement lawsuit, you can ask the court for an injunction to stop the alleged infringer from engaging in the actions that violate your patent. An injunction alone may be enough for you to achieve your goal of stopping the infringement. For example, when Amazon.com sued Barnes & Noble for violation of Amazon's patent on its one click purchase method, Amazon.com obtained an injunction against Barnes and Noble, which had the effect of shutting down Barnes & Noble's Express Lane purchasing system, and therefore achieved Amazon's objective.[6]

If you initiate a patent infringement lawsuit, the defendants are likely to fight back by seeking to prove that your patent is invalid (because if your patent is invalid, then no one can infringe it).[7] Patents are invalid if the invention is deemed obvious to people trained in the relevant technical art, or if the patent holder publicly disclosed or sold the invention more than one year before the filing of the patent application.[8] For example, eBay Inc. recently won an infringement lawsuit against it by MercExchange LLC, by showing that MercExchange's e-commerce business process patents were obvious technical improvements to people trained in the art.[9]

The U.S. Supreme Court recently made it easier to challenge the validity of someone else's patent. A licensee can now challenge validity while still paying royalties to the patent holder, which protects the licensee against the risk of a countersuit for patent infringement. Because patent infringement can result in large damages, the previous requirement that the licensee stop paying royalties to challenge patent validity kept many small, start-up companies from challenging the validity of established companies' patents. They were simply afraid of a countersuit that would cause them to go bankrupt if they lost.[10]

If you win a patent litigation lawsuit, you can obtain monetary damages and/or a permanent injunction that prohibits the infringer from using the patented technology. The amount of damages that you can obtain depends largely on the intent of the infringer. If the infringement was not deliberate, then the penalty is very lenient, usually a reasonable royalty that might be based on what the infringer would have paid the patent holder had they licensed the invention in the first place or the amount that the patent holder lost because of the infringement. Moreover, if the infringement is unintentional, the courts may require you to license the technology to the infringer in return for royalties.

It is a very different story if the infringement was willful. Then the courts can award you triple damages.[11] Willful infringement occurs if the infringer deliberately copied your patented idea, tried to conceal its effort, or acted in bad faith.[12] Therefore, the damages that you can be awarded if you win a patent litigation lawsuit can be extremely large. For example, the University of California and Eolas Technologies Inc. were awarded $565 million from Microsoft for the infringement of a software patent.[13]

The largest patent infringement penalty ever awarded went to Polaroid. In that case, Kodak had to pay $990.5 million for infringement of Polaroid's instant camera technology.[14] Moreover, Kodak had to close down a $1.5 billion manufacturing operation, lay off 700 workers, and spend $500 million to buy back cameras it had sold using the infringing technology.[15]

While the damages that you receive from winning a patent infringement lawsuit can be large, so can the costs of enforcing a patent. For example, Jet Dock Systems Inc., a company that invented a floating dry dock, has had to engage in six lawsuits to protect its patents against infringement since its founding in 1993. The cost of enforcing the company's patents—$1.2 million since founding—is large for a company that only does approximately $15 million in sales annually.[16] This makes patent litigation a major strategic issue if you run a new and small company.

It also takes a lot of time to enforce a patent. For example, it took Ron Chasteen, the inventor of a patented snowmobile fuel injection system, 11 years to win his patent infringement lawsuit against Polaris Industries.[17]

Because new and small companies must devote a large portion of their revenues and management time to enforce their patents, large, established companies often test their willingness to do so by infringing the start-ups' patents and running the risk that they might have to pay damages. Many entrepreneurs simply run out of cash or energy before they can prevail in the several-year process of enforcing a patent and then get nothing for their efforts, or settle for much less than triple damages, which they would be due if they proved willful infringement.

Patent Trolls

Patent trolls are companies whose business model is to buy up patents and seek royalties through licensing. Unlike large, established companies, such as Lucent, IBM, and Texas Instruments, that make hundreds of millions of dollars a year on licensing, patent trolls do not produce products.

The main strategy for patent trolls is litigation. Because patents give inventors the right to sue others for making or using an invention without permission, entrepreneurs can assemble a portfolio of patents and use the threat of litigation to collect royalties from potential infringers. For example, the former chief technology officer at Microsoft, Nathan Myhrvold, has created a company that has purchased several thousand software patents and uses the potential of litigation to motivate infringers to license them.[18]

Many patent trolls buy patents cheap from the creditors of bankrupt technology companies. With those patents in hand, they seek licenses from users of the patented technology, generally asking for a small royalty from companies generating high revenues from the technology. For example, they might seek a 1% royalty from a company whose product is generating $5 billion annually. Even though the trolls' odds of winning patent infringement lawsuits are small, the potential payoff is high enough to make significant profits off of their investments in the patents even if they win only occasionally.

Often companies decide that it is better to settle with patent trolls than to fight them in court. Patent trolls have a powerful strategic tool—the injunction. If they can convince a court to stop a potential infringer from producing its products or services until after an infringement lawsuit is decided, then the alleged infringer will often settle and pay a royalty to the patent troll rather than shutter its business for months or even years. For example, NTP won a $612.5 million settlement from RIM, the maker of the BlackBerry, because NTP got a federal judge to issue an injunction against RIM that would have caused them to shut down BlackBerry service while the case was decided.[19]

Should You Patent?

As you might suspect, there are advantages and disadvantages to patenting. Given these pros and cons, you need to decide whether or not to patent your inventions. To help you make informed decisions, this chapter discusses some of the important advantages and disadvantages of patenting.

Advantages of Patenting

Companies patent for a variety of different reasons. The most common reason is to prevent copying.

Barrier to Imitation

Under certain circumstances, patents can be an important barrier to imitation and a powerful mechanism to capture the returns to innovation.[1] For example, the mobile telephone company Qualcomm was founded to exploit a technology called Code Division Multiple Access (CDMA), which allows more efficient use of the radio spectrum for cellular telephones. Qualcomm obtained a patent on this technology and used the patent to protect its products, as well as to earn revenues by licensing the technology to other firms. Qualcomm has grown into a $3 billion company, successfully competing against large, established firms, such as Motorola, something it would have been unable to do if CDMA had not been patented.[2]

Legal Protection

Patents also help companies to use the legal system to protect their intellectual property. As you will see in the next chapter, it is much easier to use the legal system to enforce patents than to enforce trade secrets. Moreover, having a patent helps you to defend your firm against patent litigation by allowing you to counterclaim in an infringement lawsuit.[3]

Because patent litigation often results in court-mandated licensing or licensing from the settlement of lawsuits, the use of patents to protect intellectual property also has the benefit of creating a new source of revenue for many companies. In some cases, this source of revenue can be quite large. For example, much of IBM's $1.4 billion annual royalty flow is the result of patent litigation.[4]

Value Chain Leverage

Patents also give companies control over other firms in their value chain. By owning patents that are used by your customers or suppliers, you can influence their behavior and make them act more favorably toward you. For example, Nokia has obtained patents on cell phone speakers even though it does not produce phone components because the patents give the company leverage over its speaker supplier.[5]

Markets for Knowledge

Having a patent facilitates the sale of technology to other firms. While patented technologies can be sold to others, technologies protected by secrecy cannot. Therefore, to license a technology to another company, it helps to obtain a patent on it. Take the example of Dr. Howard Dananberg, a podiatrist in Bedford, New Hampshire, who invented a "comfortable high-heel shoe" (U.S. patent number 5,782,015). Because Dr. Dananberg lacked the assets necessary to design, manufacture, and sell shoes that were attractive to women, he sought to license his technology to companies that already produced shoes. To do this, he needed to turn over his shoe design to shoemakers, which necessitated obtaining a patent. Otherwise, if he had tried to license his invention, he would have had no protection against an unscrupulous licensee who chose to steal his design.[6]

Raising Funds

Patents help new companies raise money because they provide a verifiable source of competitive advantage. Investors can see the mechanism through which the new venture will deter imitation, reducing their uncertainty about the value of the venture. Moreover, patents offer salable assets if a new venture fails. Because investors can "take the patents to the bank" at the end of the day, they see their investments in start-ups with strong patents as partially collateralized, increasing the amount of money that they are willing to provide to them.[7]

Disadvantages of Patenting

While patents are valuable for many of the reasons just described, they also have several disadvantages.

Effectiveness at Deterring Imitation

Patents are not always effective at deterring imitation. Sometimes other firms can invent around your patents. (Inventing around is the process of coming up with something that accomplishes the same goal as the patented invention without violating the claims of the patent.) By inventing around your patents, other companies can use your invention without having to pay you royalties and without having to incur the high costs of developing the invention.

If your competitors can invent around your patents, then those patents are not worth the cost of obtaining them. Moreover, patenting might actually be doing you more harm than good because by patenting, you have to disclose the specifications of your invention, which might be the source of information that your competitors need to copy your product.

Inventing around occurs when there are multiple ways of accomplishing the same goal. For example, an imitator can often invent around an electronic device patent by changing the design of the circuitry, allowing the imitative product to satisfy customers in the same way as the innovative one but without violating the claims on the patented invention.

Thus, only for inventions for which there is a single way to accomplish a particular goal, are patents very effective at deterring imitation. For example, the patent on Symantec Corporation's antivirus software, which finds computer viruses without searching every byte of data, is effective because software engineers do not believe that there is any way other than Symantec's to find computer viruses without checking all of the data in a file.[8]

Benefits of Nondisclosure

Patenting is disadvantageous when a company will gain more from nondisclosure than from a government-granted monopoly. A patent gives you a 20-year monopoly on your invention, but secrecy might allow that monopoly to last longer. For example, the chemical formula for Coca-Cola has been maintained as a secret for over 100 years. (Because the beverage is composed of complex natural substances, it is not possible to reverse engineer and duplicate it.)[9] As a result, no other companies have been able to create beverages that taste exactly like Coke. If the formula for Coca-Cola had been patented, it would have been disclosed in the specifications of the patent. Once the monopoly on it expired, which would have been decades ago, competitors would have been able to produce soft drinks with exactly the same chemical composition (and therefore taste) as Coke.

Pace of Change

Patents are not very helpful when the pace of technological change is very fast. When technological change is very rapid, the inventions that patents protect will quickly become irrelevant. Given the time it takes to obtain patents, and the cost of patenting, you probably will not be able to earn sufficient payback to justify the investment in such patents.[10] For example, suppose your semiconductor will be obsolete in 2 years because of the pace of innovation in that industry. You might be better off just keeping it secret and using that proprietary knowledge to ensure that you, and not your competitors, will be able to develop the next generation of semiconductors. If you patent your invention, the semiconductor will be obsolete by the time that the patent issues. But once it issues, the invention will be public knowledge, and that might help your competitors to develop the next generation of semiconductors.

Moreover, to obtain a patent, you need to explain how the invention works in a way that enables a person trained in the art to make the invention. Sometimes, this information makes it possible for others to leapfrog your invention. If that is the case, you are better off keeping the invention a secret.

Difficulty Proving Infringement

Patents are not very useful when proving that others have infringed your patent, or defending it in a lawsuit, is very costly or difficult. If you cannot amass the evidence that it takes to prove that infringement actually occurred, or the fixed costs of defending a patent are so high that it does not pay to protect it through the court system, then you will not get enough of a return on your investment in a patent to justify its cost.[11] For example, it may be very difficult to prove that someone infringed a surgical method that you invented, such as a type of incision used in cataract surgery, because there are no sales of physical objects, like drugs or devices, which would show that your method was used.[12] As a result, you might not want to waste your money trying to patent the surgical method.

Effectiveness of Patents in Different Industries

Patents are not equally effective in all industries. In general, they tend to be more effective in industries in which the core technology is biological or chemical, and less effective in industries in which the core technology is mechanical or electrical.[13] Why? The reason has to do with the difficulty of accomplishing the same goals through different technical means. For mechanical or electrical devices, you can make slight modifications to the design and accomplish the same goal, but you cannot do this with things that are biological or chemical. For example, a drug has a very precise molecular structure, and slight alterations will often transform the drug from something beneficial to something harmful, while relatively major changes to the structure of electronic circuitry often do not alter an electronic device's effectiveness.

Researchers have examined how effective patents are in different industries. In industries like drugs and chemicals, patents are very effective at protecting new products, but in industries such as cosmetics or pulp and paper, they are not.[14] These differences in patent effectiveness explain why obtaining patents is crucial to generating high financial returns in industries in which patents are very effective, such as pharmaceuticals.[15] It also explains why start-ups in some industries, like biotechnology, often specialize in technology development and do not build assets across the different parts of the value chain, relying instead on licensing to capture value from innovation.

Secrecy

You can deter imitation by keeping things secret and reducing the diffusion of information about your products or services or how you produce them. For example, suppose that you have discovered a chemical that makes an excellent fertilizer. If you run a fertilizer company, you might not want other people to know that you have identified this chemical. If your competitors and potential competitors do not know that the key to your fertilizer lies in the use of a particular chemical, then they will not understand that they need to gain access to that chemical to compete with you successfully. Therefore, they will not seek to obtain access to that resource, and they will not be able to imitate your operations successfully.

When Does Secrecy Work?

Efforts to mitigate imitation by keeping information about a new product or service secret work best under certain conditions. First, they work better when there are few sources of the information about the new product or service. To imitate your product or service, a competitor needs access to the information that makes copying the innovation possible. While your competitors can obtain this information from you, they can also get it from third parties. Your efforts to keep things secret are not going to be very effective if third parties readily provide this information to your competitors. Therefore, if only you know the information necessary to imitate your product or service, then your product or service is less likely to be copied.

This is why it is easier for Coca-Cola to keep other companies from copying its soft drink formula than it is for your local dry cleaner to keep its dry cleaning formula secret. Even if your local dry cleaner never told anyone the formula for its dry cleaning solution, you could obtain it from any of thousands of other dry cleaners. However, if the few executives at Coca-Cola who know the formula to classic Coke do not tell you what it is, then you are going to have no way of knowing it.

Second, secrecy is more effective when a new product or service is complex. Imitation involves understanding how to copy a new product or service, not just having access to formulas or blueprints. The more complex a product or service is, the harder it is for people to figure out how to duplicate it. Complexity affects people's understanding of the order in which tasks need to be undertaken and the difficulty of choreographing the joint efforts of different people. Take, for example, the challenge of assembling a child's toy. Even if you have the instructions, it is much harder to make the product just as the manufacturer has intended when the product is made up of hundreds of pieces than when it is made up of only a couple of pieces.[1]

Third, secrecy is more effective when the process of creating a new product or service is poorly understood. To imitate your activities, people have to understand what you are doing. The fewer competitors that can actually understand what you are doing, the fewer that will be capable of imitating your products, and the less imitation there will be. For example, suppose that you developed a new method for keeping storm drains clean by flushing them with a chemical mixture at certain temperatures. If the process of creating this new chemical solution was poorly understood (e.g., very precise amounts of the chemicals have to be combined at exactly the right moment under the right temperature for unknown reasons), then few people would be able to imitate this product, and your company would capture the profits from providing it.

Fourth, secrecy works best when the information that is being kept secret involves tacit knowledge—knowledge about how to do something that is not documented in written form. For example, a plant manager's knowledge of how to keep an assembly line running at high speed through a sense of where to position different workers with different skills and a sales person's knowledge of how to close sales by timing the introduction of personal comments into a discussion are both examples of tacit knowledge.

It is easier to imitate a well-codified process than a tacitly understood one because imitation of a codified process only requires access to the document outlining the process, whereas imitation of a tacitly understood process requires the imitator to gain access to the person who holds that information in his head. Most of the time, it is easier to gain control of a document about a process than to gain control of a person who knows about it.[2] Take, for example, the case of expertise in boiler repair. If that knowledge is held in documentary form by a company in Michigan, then a company in Ohio could get control of that information and move it to Ohio more easily than it could if the knowledge was tacit and held in the minds of the Michigan firm's employees. To copy the tacit knowledge, competitors would need to hire the employees of the Michigan firm and get them to move to Ohio to imitate the product or service.

Moreover, when knowledge is tacit, its transfer must take place through face-to-face meetings between people. In contrast, when things are codified, knowledge can be transferred by handing a blueprint or a formula to others.[3] Because knowledge spreads much faster if the transfer is not limited to direct contact between people, codified knowledge tends to spread very quickly and is harder to keep secret than information that is not written down.

Fifth, secrecy works better when there are limited numbers of people capable of understanding the information that is being kept secret. The fewer people who have the skills and abilities to use the information that creates your new product's value, the fewer people who can figure out how to imitate what you are doing, even if the knowledge that you are keeping secret leaks out. Researchers Lynne Zucker and Michael Darby at the University of California, Los Angeles, business school have shown this to be true for new biotechnology companies. They learned that the new biotechnology firms founded to exploit the technical expertise of leading scientists often were successful because competition was limited to the handful of people who also had the skills to exploit the cutting-edge scientific techniques that they used.[4]

Sixth, secrecy works better for processes, inputs, and materials than for products. Why? You sell your product in the marketplace. That makes the product itself observable-in-use. (In fact, the more observable-in-use a product is, the less it can be kept secret. This is also why it is hard to keep secret certain processes, such as techniques for providing customer service.)[5] Moreover, competitors can buy your product and reverse engineer it to figure out how it works. [6] These things make it harder for you to keep the composition of your product secret than it is for you to keep secret the production processes used to make the product. Therefore, processes make better secrets than products.

Trade Secrets

Trade secrecy is a special case of all efforts to keep a new product or service secret. In the United States, trade secrets are governed by state law,[7] primarily the Uniform Trade Secrets Act, which is in force in 44 states.[8] This act defines a trade secret as "information including a formula, pattern, compilation, program, device, method, technique, or process that derives independent economic value, actual or potential, from not being generally known, and not being readily ascertainable by proper means by, other persons." Examples of trade secrets include chemical processes; customer databases; food recipes; computer source code, manufacturing processes, architectural designs, vendor lists, and marketing plans; and sources of raw materials, design manuals, pricing policies, and blueprints.[9] For example, one of the most valuable trade secrets today is Google's Web page ranking algorithm, which makes its search engine better than others.

Trade secrecy laws provide for legal remedies if someone benefits from your trade secret without your consent. If you believe that someone else has improperly obtained a trade secret, you can sue to collect damages for your loss and obtain an injunction to stop further use of the secret. These remedies are available to you regardless of whether the party disclosing the trade secret was bound by duty of confidentiality, had signed a nondisclosure agreement, obtained the information illegally, obtained the information from someone who did not have authorization to disclose it, or learned the information by accident but knew it was a trade secret. [10]

Conditions to Have a Trade Secret

Three conditions must be met for the courts to hold that something is a trade secret. First, the information must be known only by people in your company. Information that is known generally in an industry, such as standard manufacturing processes, or information that can be generated from data that are known in an industry, cannot be a trade secret.[11] Moreover, you cannot claim that the general skills that your employees learn on the job are trade secrets because that would preclude them from being able to take new jobs and use the skills that they learned working for you at their new employers.[12]

Second, the information must have economic value. For something to be a trade secret, it must generate a competitive advantage that would be lost if your competitors made use of it. This means that you must be able to document that what you term a trade secret is central to how your company derives value and provides an advantage over your competition in the marketplace. You should note that this standard is stricter than for a patent, where all you have to do is prove infringement to collect damages.

Third, you must take reasonable measures to keep the information secret. This means that you have to adopt "secrecy policies" to ensure that people do not accidentally access the secret information. Your employees need to know what information is secret and that secret information is limited to only those personnel who need it. Moreover, those personnel who need access to the information must agree, in writing, to keep it confidential. Furthermore, you need to use physical mechanisms, such limiting the access of nonemployees to your facilities, locking files, requiring computer passwords, and so on to keep the information from getting out.[13]

Take, for example, the efforts by Kentucky Fried Chicken (KFC) to keep the recipe for its fried chicken a trade secret. The recipe is kept in a vault at the company's headquarters and only a few people know what it is. Those employees who know the formula are required by the terms of their employment to keep the recipe secret. Moreover, two different companies supply the herbs and spices to KFC, but each one is allowed to create only part of the ingredients and neither company is known to the other.[14]

Secrecy as a Strategy

You might choose secrecy as your basic approach to protecting intellectual property. This choice may stem from a preference for trade secrets over patents as the basis for competitive advantage (the two sources of intellectual property protection are mutually exclusive, necessitating a choice), perhaps because trade secrecy offers a longer time horizon of protection or because it does not disclose information to your competitors. Or it may occur because you have a product for which secrecy is particularly effective: It is created through a process that is poorly understood, complex, and based on tacit knowledge for which there are few sources of information and a limited number of people who can comprehend it. You might even focus on secrecy to generate customer interest in your products and services because people are often more interested in things that they cannot know about than things that they can.

Apple Computer is an example of a high technology company that focuses strongly on secrecy. (A former CEO, John Scully, was fond of using the phrase, "loose lips sink ships.") The company rarely discloses its plans for new products and compartmentalizes development efforts so that employees working on new products rarely have information about the entire product. The company vigorously maintains efforts to limit disclosure, suing employees who leak information about forthcoming products, and Web sites that publish such information. It creates lists of employees who have been given access to information about new product plans, even watermarking documents with the recipient's name and using different code numbers for different departments to better track the source of any leak. Access to buildings in Apple's headquarters is even limited to the part of the complex in which employees work.[15]

While secrecy-focused strategies, such as Apple's, have many advantages, these benefits come at a cost. As was mentioned earlier, maintaining trade secrets is costly. It requires the adoption of secrecy policies and reduces the level of informal exchange of information among your employees, which hinders your ability to develop new products and processes. Maintaining trade secrets also hinders your efforts to work with other companies, which by necessity, lack adequate information to serve as effective partners. Moreover, it inhibits efforts to sell products to many business customers who need to know about new products long in advance of their release to fit them into their own plans. Finally, maintaining trade secrets risks the independent discovery and exploitation of your inventions. Competitors who independently and legally obtain technology that you maintain as a trade secret are free to use it, even though they would be barred from doing so if you patented the technology.

For example, if other companies figure out how to create your product through legal means—reading your publications, talking to your suppliers or customers, or reverse engineering your product—nothing would stop them from making and selling exactly the same product as you.

Nondisclosure Agreements

Trade secrecy is enhanced by having people sign nondisclosure agreements that are crafted by lawyers who know the details of employment law. These agreements are important; you cannot make a case that you are keeping information secret unless your employees understand that they are expected to refrain from disclosing information.

Effective nondisclosure agreements must meet certain conditions. The agreements must specify exactly what information is to be kept secret and cannot state that all information that employees learn during their employment is confidential. Moreover, the agreement must provide consideration. That is, employees must receive something of value, such as their salaries, in return for nondisclosure. Furthermore, the agreement must specify legitimate uses for the information, including identifying those people to whom the information can be disclosed and how the information may be used to perform a job. Lastly, the agreement must state what must be done with any documents or materials that are transferred to the employee, both during employment and after the termination of an employment relationship.[16]

Enforcing Nondisclosure Agreements

To enforce nondisclosure agreements, you need to be willing to sue your employees and others who help them because the only remedies for violation of nondisclosure agreements come through legal action. Many companies do this. For example, Biomec Inc., a Cleveland, Ohio, medical device company, sued a former employee claiming that he violated his confidentiality agreement when he moved to rival Cleveland Medical Devices; and Wal-Mart sued Drugstore.com and the venture capital firm Kleiner Perkins when Drugstore.com hired former Wal-Mart employees who had developed that company's system for Internet retailing.[17]

While the easiest case to make for violation of a nondisclosure agreement occurs when your employees take documents that belong to your company, you can make a case that they violated their nondisclosure agreements if they take only uncodified knowledge. For example, IBM recently settled a lawsuit with Compuware Corp. in which Compuware alleged that IBM had violated Compuware's trade secrets for file management and error detection software by hiring former Compuware employees to speed the development of software for its mainframe computers. In this case, Compuware claimed that its former employees had signed confidentiality agreements and then disclosed technical knowledge and knowledge of customer preferences to IBM.[18]

Noncompete Agreements

Trade secrecy is enhanced by having your employees sign noncompete agreements, which bar them from working for competitors for a period of time after their employment has ended, because these agreements keep employees from moving to rivals while their company-specific knowledge still has value. For example, Microsoft successfully forced a start-up company named CrossGain to lay off 20 former Microsoft employees until the expiration of their noncompete agreements, as a way to protect its intellectual property.[19]

Enforcing Noncompete Agreements

As with nondisclosure agreements, you need to be prepared to go to court to enforce your noncompete agreements. For example, Patio Enclosures Inc. had to take Four Seasons Solar Products to court for hiring a former Patio Enclosures employee who had signed a noncompete agreement that barred him from employment at a competing firm for 2 years.[20]

While noncompete agreements help you to protect your company's intellectual property, they are hard to enforce. These agreements need to be of limited length and limited geographic breadth because they will be declared invalid if they keep people from earning a living in their chosen field.[21] For example, ExxonMobil's noncompete agreement cannot preclude a petroleum engineer from working at another oil company after leaving ExxonMobil. Moreover, in many states, you must give employees some benefit, such as a bonus or a higher salary, in return for asking them to sign a noncompete agreement;[22] while in other states, such as California, you cannot enforce these agreements at all.[23]

Ownership of Intellectual Property

Related to the issue of nondisclosure and noncompete agreements is the issue of who owns the rights to technologies that employees develop during their employment at a company. These rights reside with employees unless you require them to assign the rights to you. Of course, most large companies do just this, which keeps many people from quitting and starting new companies to exploit technologies that they developed while working elsewhere. For example, Jeff Hawkins, the founder of Palm Inc. computing, patented an algorithm for pattern recognition software when he was on academic leave from GRiD systems, his employer. Although he owned the patent, and his licensing agreement with GRiD allowed him to use the algorithm in noncompeting products, he did not have the rights to the improvements to the C-language enhancements he had made while he was a GRiD employee. As a result, he needed to work around this intellectual property to develop the Palm personal digital assistant (PDA).[24]

Copyrights

A copyright is a legal protection given to the authors of original literary, musical, or artistic works.[1] It gives the right to reproduce, display, or produce derivative works from the protected item. It also gives the right to sue to collect damages if someone else infringes the copyright from the time the work was created until 70 years after the author's death (or 95 years after publication for works for hire, which will be discussed later in this chapter). Infringement occurs if another party duplicates, displays, produces, or distributes the work; or gives, rents, or lends it to others.

What Can Be Copyrighted?

Many things can be protected by copyright, including books, movies, software, music, other recordings, databases, plays, pantomimes, dance, sculptures, graphics, and architectural designs.[2] For example, the Lego Group has used copyrights to protect the appearance of its standard, eight-studded brick against imitation.[3] The thing that you want to protect does not need to be novel or even lawful to receive copyright protection. For example, Napster's software copyright still held even after the file-sharing service was deemed unlawful.[4]

However, there are some limitations on what can be protected by copyright. First, the thing being protected has to be tangible. Thus, you cannot copyright an impromptu speech, but you can copyright a written one. Second, titles and names cannot be protected by copyright; these things are protected by trademarks. Third, slogans, ideas, methods, principles, discoveries, or things composed of common property, such as calendars, cannot be copyrighted.[5] Fourth, it has to be a finished product; ideas cannot be copyrighted.

Who Gets a Copyright and How Do They Get It?

So who can get a copyright? A copyright can be obtained by the author of any completed original artistic, literary, or musical work, unless the work is done for hire. Work-for-hire is a technical term for work that is done under the scope of a person's employment or under a written agreement between the author and the person contracting for the work, which requests that the work be done on the contractor's behalf. If the work is done for hire, then the copyright goes to the entity commissioning the work. For example, you could hire your neighbor to write some software for the insurance claims adjusting business that you are starting and the copyright on that software would then belong to you.[6]

You can obtain a copyright without taking any action other than putting the intellectual property into tangible form (e.g., writing something on paper or recording it on a DVD or CD). Alternatively, you can apply for copyright protection from the U.S. Patent and Trademark Office (USPTO). While applying for a copyright is not necessary, it does provide a couple of important advantages. Most notably, you need to have a registered copyright to file a lawsuit to protect your copyrighted intellectual property, so registration is useful in the event that you want to sue someone.

Enforcement Through Litigation

If you think that someone has improperly used your copyrighted materials, you can take them to court and sue them for infringement. Because plaintiffs in a copyright infringement lawsuit rarely have direct evidence of the actual incidence of copying (of course, having photos of people in the act of copying your copyrighted material and distributing it would strengthen your case!), the courts usually infer that copying has occurred if the new work is substantially similar to the copyrighted work and the defendant had access to the copyrighted work.

If you win a copyright infringement lawsuit, the court will award you damages. The size of those damages depends on the intent of the infringers, how much money they made, how they made their money, and how their actions affected your business. For example, if the infringers charged others for your copyrighted material, then the size of the damages that you can receive will be greater than if they gave away your material for free. Also, the size of the damage settlement will be larger if the infringers reduced the commercial value of your property through their actions.

If the court determines that the infringers' imitation was intentional, then you can collect triple the value of your loss as damages. So it is important to affix the copyright symbol (©) to your material. Doing so allows the court to reject any claim by an infringer that he or she did not know the material was copyrighted and innocently infringed.[7]

If you believe that someone has infringed your copyright, you can have a court issue an injunction, stopping that party from using your copyrighted material while the case is being decided. However, if you believe that your copyrighted material has been infringed, you need to take action quickly. The statute of limitations on copyrights only lasts for 3 years.

Recent Developments to Strengthen Copyrights

Although copyrights were originally intended to protect written documents, in recent years, most of their growth has been as a means of protecting sound and images (as well as computer software). Now such things as video recordings of Super Bowl games and Web casts of the weather outside of college dorms are routinely copyrighted.

However, software is easier to copy than books and other printed material because duplicating and distributing multiple copies of a book takes more time and money than duplicating and distributing a piece of software. To deter copying and illegal distribution, software companies impose very restrictive end user license agreements (EULAs). By severely limiting how their customers can use their product, software companies strengthen their position against violators of their copyrights.

Unfortunately for copyright holders, the development of network technology to share digital files has led to other issues. File sharing technology has made it easy to copy musical recordings, leading to the decline in sales of music CDs. This has prompted the record labels to sue anyone who does anything that lets users get around their copyrights. For example, several record labels sued XM Satellite Radio because XM's Inno device allows users to record, store, and create playlists of songs that they have heard on XM. The record labels claim that the use of the Inno device violates the copyrights to their songs by allowing people to obtain a recording of it without paying a royalty.[8]

Similarly, the record labels sued Napster, charging that the company violated the copyrights of recording artists, and caused them financial loss, by making it possible for people to exchange digital music files without paying royalties. The record labels' argument was that Napster created a market in which other people could avoid paying royalties on copyrighted songs, thus enabling infringement.[9] (The copyright issue was not settled in this case because Napster was forced to shut down when the judge in the case issued an injunction banning Napster from offering the service until the courts had decided the case.[10] However, many observers believe that file-sharing networks will not be able to claim "fair use" of copyrighted material.)

While the recording industry was able to use the court system to enforce its copyrights against the first generation of peer-to-peer networks like Napster, they face a more difficult time with second generation peer-to-peer networks that do not use a central server for file sharing. The use of peer-to-peer networks spreads the copyright violation across numerous parties and makes the value of their infringement too small to justify the use of lawsuits as a way to stop it.[11]

Recently, laws have been enacted to let companies use physical tools, such as embedded authentication chips, to make it more difficult for people to copy a piece of intellectual property. For example, the Audio Home Recording Act of 1992 requires that all digital recording devices include a Serial Copy Management System, which permits originals but not copies to be duplicated. And the Digital Millennium Copyright Act (DMCA) made it illegal to circumvent a technological device that is used to prevent duplication of copyrighted material. [12]

However, the use of copy protection software to prevent sharing of intellectual property has had problematic side effects. It limits the devices that customers can use to play legitimately purchased recordings or even causes damage to computers that play the recordings.[13] For example, Sony BMG recently had to reimburse its customers more than $100 each for computers damaged by hidden antipiracy software that Sony BMG had placed on their CDs because the software created security risks and was hard to uninstall.[14]

Efforts to strengthen copyrights have had other adverse effects as well. They have diluted the concept of "fair use" of copyrighted material. As a result, it is becoming more difficult to make noncommercial use of copyrighted materials. Second, these efforts have hindered the natural process by which innovators build on the work of others by requiring them to obtain the rights to use any copyrighted material to build on it.

Software Copyrights

Copyrights have become an important mechanism to protect software. While the mathematical formulas and equations underlying software programs are not copyrightable, nor are the ideas or methods behind them, copyrights can be used to protect many parts of computer software, including source code, object code, microcode, and screen displays.[15] For example, ConnectU.com, a social networking Web site, uses copyrights to protect its source code.[16]

While copyrights provide some intellectual property protection for software, they are not an ideal form of protection for this medium because they only protect the expression of ideas, not the concepts underlying those ideas. Ideas can often be expressed in a variety of different ways, allowing someone to reverse engineer a piece of software and then write a new piece of software that works around the copyright by expressing the same idea in a different way. If a defendant in a software copyright case can show that they created a work independently and expressed an idea in a different way from the holder of the copyright, then there is no copyright violation.[17]

Moreover, demonstrating the infringement of a software copyright is not easy to do directly, making them difficult to enforce. Because it is impossible to show an exact linkage between the expression of an idea and the processes to express it, courts have had to interpret the "look and feel" of software to determine whether copyright infringement has occurred. Of course, this reliance on "look and feel" to determine infringement makes it harder to know if infringement has actually occurred. [18]

On the other hand, software copyrights provide additional intellectual property protection to that provided by software patents. A wider variety of software programs can be copyrighted than can be patented because any originally authored work presented in tangible form can be protected by a copyright, whereas only novel, nonobvious, and useful inventions can be protected by a patent. Copyrights also are much easier to obtain than patents and are, consequently, a much less expensive form of protection. Furthermore, copyrights offer 70 years of protection from the time of the author's death, whereas patents offer only 20 years of protection from the time of invention.[19]

Trademarks

Trademarks are devices used to identify the provider of a product or service.[1] While they offer much less intellectual property protection than patents, copyrights, or trade secrets, they do help companies to protect their brand names. For example, the Intel Inside® trademark helps Intel build its brand by making it easier for that company to differentiate itself from competitors.

In addition, trademarks can be used as leverage to drive other forms of strategic advantage. For example, Cisco recently settled a lawsuit with Apple Computer Inc. over violation of its iPhone trademark. Cisco wanted Apple to make its iPod and iPhone products compatible with non-Apple products. By blocking Apple's use of the iPhone name, Cisco forced Apple to concede on the issue of compatibility.[2]

Because consumers associate particular trademarks or servicemarks with the quality of the products or services that companies provide, some trademarks are quite valuable. For example, the Microsoft trademark is now worth $60 billion.[3] Therefore, learning how trademarks work and how they protect intellectual property is an important part of technology strategy.

What Can Be Trademarked?

A trademark can be obtained on any word, number, symbol, phrase, color, design, or even smell that distinguishes the products and services of one company from those of another. For example, Nike has trademarked its "swoosh" symbol, while Porsche AG has trademarked the numerical sequence "911."[4]

However, not everything can be trademarked. For a word, number, symbol, phrase, color, design, or smell to be appropriate as a trademark, it cannot describe the product or service that a company provides. For example, a supermarket cannot trademark the word "carrot" because that word is descriptive of the products sold at a supermarket. However, an airline could trademark the name "carrot" because carrots are not descriptive of what airlines do. A common word, such as "house," cannot be trademarked. However, what is a common word lies in the interpretation of the courts. A federal appeals court recently upheld *Entrepreneur Magazine*'s trademark on the word "entrepreneur," allowing that company to block the use of that word by others.

Ironically, the fact that another party has trademarked a word, number, symbol, phrase, color, design, or smell does not mean that you cannot use the same one. A trademark can be used by more than one company if customers would not be confused about the identity of the provider of the product or what the product is used for, and if the use by a second party does not dilute the value of the trademark. Typically, this means that a trademark can be used by two companies if they sell different types of products and services (e.g., airplanes and vegetables) through different channels. For example, Apple Computer and Apple Records are both able to have trademarks with the word "apple" in them because Beatles songs and personal computers are very different products and are sold through different marketing channels. However, as Apple Computer moves further into the music business, it may face problems using its trademarked name for that business because the name might then cause confusion among customers as to the provider of the product.

Obtaining a Trademark

So how do you get a trademark? In common law countries, such as the United States, you get a trademark by using the word, phrase, symbol, design, or smell, or by registering that mark with the U.S. Patent and Trademark Office (USPTO).[5] The process of registering a trade or service mark is very simple. You just send an application to the USPTO along with a drawing of the mark and the payment of the fee for the relevant category of mark.

However, before you send in your application and pay the money to register a trademark, you probably want to conduct a trademark search. The USPTO is not going to give you a trademark to something that violates another company's mark. Conducting a trademark search will minimize the chances that you will select something that infringes another mark, and reduces the likelihood that you will select something that cannot be trademarked.

Although you will not get trademark or servicemark rights from the USPTO until you use a mark, and you do not need to register the mark to enforce it, you probably want to go down the registration route when you seek trademark protection. Registration provides a record of your claim of ownership of the mark, which is useful to signal your actions to competitors. In addition, you cannot sue to protect your trademark or servicemark, or collect triple damages in the case of infringement, until the mark has been registered.[6] Furthermore, registration makes it easier to obtain trademark or servicemark rights in other countries.[7]

Enforcing a Trademark

Once you have registered a trademark, your ownership of it lasts for 10 years and can be renewed as long as the trademark is in use and has not been invalidated.[8] However, 5 years after you have obtained the trademark, you will need to file an affidavit with the USPTO attesting that the mark is still in use. If you do not do this, your trademark can be cancelled.

Trademarks can be invalidated by the USPTO in one of three ways: through cancellation proceedings, through abandonment, or through generic meaning. Cancellation occurs when the owner of the mark fails to attest to its continued use.

Abandonment occurs when someone else can show that the trademark owner has stopped using a mark. For example, in the recent dispute between Cisco and Apple Computer over the trademark "iPhone," Apple Computer sought to show that Cisco did not sell iPhone branded products for a period of time, thus indicating that Cisco abandoned the trademark.[9] The potential for abandonment is why trademark holders fight hard to protect their trademarks. For example, Entrepreneur Magazine Inc. fought to exert its rights to the trademark "entrepreneur" against a variety of small companies not because it thought it would obtain any significant royalties from enforcing the trademark, but to defend the use of the mark against other companies that claimed that *Entrepreneur Magazine* had abandoned it.

Generic use occurs when the mark no longer represents a specific product or service and ends up representing a general category of products or services (as occurred, for example, with the once trademarked term "escalator").[10] Once a trademark becomes a generic term, it reverts to the public domain and anyone can use it. That is why Bayer works hard to ensure that Aspirin® is not used to refer to all pain medications. If that were to occur, the word could no longer be trademarked because it would no longer distinguish Bayer's product from those of other companies.

Like other forms of intellectual property protection, trademarks are enforced through legal action. Trademark owners can sue to prevent both infringement and dilution of their trademarks.[11] Infringement occurs when a competitor's use of a trademark causes confusion among customers about the provider of a product. For example, VOIP start-up, Vonage, has sued AT&T claiming that the name of AT&T's VOIP service, CallVantage violates its trademark because the name is too similar to its own.

Dilution occurs when another party's use of a word, phrase, symbol, design, or smell lowers the value of a company's trademark. For example, American Express was able to stop a limousine service from using the name "American Express" by showing that its trademark's value was reduced by that action.[12]

You need to protect your trademarks. Failure to take legal action to enforce your rights can result in the loss of the trademark through abandonment. Unfortunately, taking legal action costs money, and many organizations fail to protect valuable trademarks. For example, Metropolitan Transit Authority (MTA) in New York City has trademarked its circular route symbols for the A, D, F, 1, 4, and 7 trains. However, many companies frequently violate MTA's trademarks by making unauthorized T-shirts—or, in the case of Eli Zabar's food emporium, rectangular cookies with hard icing designed to look like New York City MetroCards. Although MTA has written letters to many of the trademark violators, it lacks the legal staff to go to court to enforce its trademarks and has allowed the value of those trademarks to deteriorate.[13]

Start-ups face a greater challenge than large, established companies in developing an effective strategy toward the management of trademarks. Because small, new companies are often cash constrained, they face the dilemma of whether challenging—and winning—a trademark infringement lawsuit is worthwhile. The start-up might win the suit against a deep pocketed competitor but be driven out of business by the legal effort. Take, for example, the case of Haute Diggity Dog, a dog toy manufacturer. They created dog toys shaped like handbags, called "Chewy Vuiton." Louis Vuitton, makers of the handbags that Haute Diggity Dog was parodying, sued them for degrading the value of Louis Vuitton's trademark. While Haute Diggity Dog won the lawsuit, it lost a lot of distributors because Louis Vuitton sent cease-and-desist letters to the retailers during the lawsuit, causing the retailers to stop carrying Haute Diggity Dog's products.[14]

Domain Names

Domain names are the names used on Web sites to identify an organization providing a good or service. Domain names have become an increasingly popular form of intellectual property protection, as companies do more and more business over the Web.

Domain names are registered by the Internet Corporation for Assigned Names and Numbers (ICANN) to the first party to seek registration for that name.[15] As with trademarks, it is useful to conduct a search before trying to register a domain name to make sure that you can obtain the name that you would like to use. You can do this at the ICANN Web site (www.icann.org).

The protection of domain names is similar to the protection of trademarks. However, two important distinctions exist: First, because geographic regions are not meaningful in cyberspace, companies in different places are not permitted to use the same domain name, though they are permitted to use the same trademark.[16] Second, unlike with trademarks, common words can be used as domain names. For example, Proctor & Gamble has obtained the domain name "cavities.com."[17]

Your domain name also cannot adversely affect another company's business. If it does, the company whose business has been hurt can sue you for control of your domain name. For example, Universal Tube and Rollerform Equipment Corporation has sued YouTube for the rights to the www.youtube.com domain name because the volume of people going to Universal Tube's Web site www.utube.com when looking for www.youtube.com has caused Universal Tube's Web servers to crash repeatedly.

The enforcement of a domain name occurs in a similar way to the enforcement of a trademark. If you believe that someone else has infringed your domain name or has taken action to lower its value, you can sue the offending party.[18] For example, Sir Ratan N. Tata of Bombay, India, the leader of India's Tata group of companies (which includes Tata Steel, Tata Engineering, Tata Power, Tata Chemicals, Tata Finance, Tata Power, Tata Tea, and Tata Sons Ltd.) and the Sir Rata Tata Trust, sued a New Jersey porn site in 1999, and obtained an injunction against the latter's use of the Internet domain name BODACIOUSTATAS.COM because the New Jersey company's use of the domain name harmed the reputation, and hence the value, of Sir Ratan's companies. [19]

However, enforcement of domain name infringement is often more difficult than enforcement of trademark infringement because domain names operate in cyberspace. As a result, it is often difficult to determine the legal jurisdiction in which to sue an offender, and when that jurisdiction can be determined, it is often a place that does not strongly enforce intellectual property laws, making it hard for you to stop the offending action or collect damages.[20]

Conclusion

Most companies can easily and quickly imitate their competitors' products and services. Therefore, firms need to obtain intellectual property protection. This book has examined the legal mechanisms to protect your intellectual property. It has defined a patent and explained what characteristics of an invention are necessary to obtain one. It has identified the different types of patents and explained what they protect. It has identified the key parts of a patent and explained what they do. It has outlined the trends over time in the expansion of what is patentable and discussed the pros and cons of these trends. It has defined patent infringement and explained how patent owners can use the legal system to enforce their patent rights. It has discussed the benefits and limitations of patenting, and explained when patenting makes the most sense.

The book has also identified the role that secrecy plays in protecting intellectual property. It has explained when secrecy tends to be an effective mechanism for deterring imitation. It has defined a trade secret and explained what characteristics are necessary for something to be a trade secret. It has explained why nondisclosure agreements are an important part of efforts to maintain trade secrecy. It has defined a copyright and explained how intellectual property can be protected by copyright. It has described how a copyright is obtained. It has defined a trademark and explained why and how trademarks are beneficial. Finally, it has described how a trademark is obtained and protected.

Now that you have this information, you should be able to manage your intellectual property assets in ways that benefit your company. Good luck in that effort.

Notes

Introduction

1. McGavock, D. (2002). Intangible assets: A ticking time bomb. *Chief Executive*. Retrieved from http://findarticles.com/p/articles/mi_m4070/is_2002_Nov/ai_94145235

Why You Need Intellectual Property Protection

1. Levin, R., Klevorick, A., Nelson, R., & Winter, S. (1987). Appropriating the returns from industrial research and development. *Brookings Papers on Economic Activity, 3*, 783–832.

2. Mansfield, E. (1985). How rapidly does industrial technology leak out? *Journal of Industrial Economics, 34*(2), 217–223.

3. Levin, R., Klevorick, A., Nelson, R., & Winter, S. (1987). Appropriating the returns from industrial research and development. *Brookings Papers on Economic Activity, 3*, 783–832.

4. Levin, R., Klevorick, A., Nelson, R., & Winter, S. (1987). Appropriating the returns from industrial research and development. *Brookings Papers on Economic Activity, 3*, 783–832.

5. Levin, R., Klevorick, A., Nelson, R., & Winter, S. (1987). Appropriating the returns from industrial research and development. *Brookings Papers on Economic Activity, 3*, 783–832.

What Is Patentable?

1. Jaffe, A., & Lerner, J. (2004). *Innovation and its discontents*. Princeton, NJ: Princeton University Press.

2. Lemley, M., & Shapiro, C. (2005). Probabilistic patents. *Journal of Economic Perspectives, 19*(2), 75–98.

3. Winter, S. (2000). Appropriating the gains from innovation. In G. Day & P. Schoemaker (Eds.), *Wharton on managing emerging technologies* (pp. 242–266). New York: John Wiley.

4. U.S. Department of Commerce. (1992). *General information concerning patents*. Washington, DC: U.S. Government Printing Office.

5. Kesan, J. (2000). Intellectual property protection and agricultural biotechnology. *The American Behavioral Scientist, 44*(3), 464–503.

6. Etherton, S. (2002). *Let's talk patents.* Tempe, AZ: Rocket Science Press.

7. Yoffie, D. (2003). Intellectual property and strategy. *Harvard Business School Note*, No. 9-704-493.

8. Schilling, M. (2005). *Strategic management of technological innovation.* New York: McGraw-Hill.

9. Yoffie, D. (2003). Intellectual property and strategy. *Harvard Business School Note*, No. 9-704-493.

10. Munoz, S. (2005, April 5). Patent no. 6,004,596: Peanut butter and jelly sandwich. *Wall Street Journal*, pp. B1, B9.

11. Yoffie, D. (2003). Intellectual property and strategy. *Harvard Business School Note*, No. 9-704-493.

12. Jaffe, A., & Lerner, J. (2004). *Innovation and our discontents.* Princeton, NJ: Princeton University Press.

13. Sandoval, G. (2005, August 17). Apple-Microsoft duke out iPod fight in patent office. *The Plain Dealer*, p. C2.

14. Silverman, A. (1999). The forfeiture of U.S. patent rights by placing an invention on sale. *JOM, 51*(2), 64.

15. U.S. Department of Commerce. (1992). *General information concerning patents.* Washington, DC: U.S. Government Printing Office.

16. Etherton, S. (2002). *Let's talk patents.* Tempe, AZ: Rocket Science Press.

17. Jaffe, A., & Lerner, J. (2004). *Innovation and its discontents.* Princeton, NJ: Princeton University Press.

18. Kesan, J. (2000). Intellectual property protection and agricultural biotechnology. *The American Behavioral Scientist, 44*(3), 464–503.

19. Jaffe, A., & Lerner, J. (2004). *Innovation and its discontents.* Princeton, NJ: Princeton University Press.

20. Bercowitz, L. (2000). Patent law changes: What you should know. *Research Technology Management, 43*(2), 5.

21. Fuerst, O., & Geiger, U. (2003). *From concept to Wall Street: A complete guide to entrepreneurship and venture capital.* New York: Financial Times, Prentice Hall.

22. U.S. Department of Commerce. (1992). *General information concerning patents.* Washington, DC: U.S. Government Printing Office.

23. Flandez, R. (2005, May 9). Get a patent. *Wall Street Journal*, pp. R9, R11.

24. U.S. Department of Commerce. (1992). *General information concerning patents.* Washington, DC: U.S. Government Printing Office.

The Parts of a Patent

1. Etherton, S. (2002). *Let's talk patents*. Tempe, AZ: Rocket Science Press.

2. Montgomery, C. (2004, July 20). Drive-in dry-dock. *The Plain Dealer*, pp. C1, C6.

3. Etherton, S. (2002). *Let's talk patents*. Tempe, AZ: Rocket Science Press.

4. Regalado, A. (2004). Nanotechnology patents surge as companies vie to stake claim. *Wall Street Journal*, June 18, pp. A1, A2.

5. Vara, V. (2006, July 27). Friendster patent on linking Web friends could hurt rivals. *Wall Street Journal*, pp. B1, B4.

6. Flandez, R. (2005, May 9). Get a patent. *Wall Street Journal*, pp. R9, R11.

7. Regalado, A. (2004). Nanotechnology patents surge as companies vie to stake claim. *Wall Street Journal*, June 18, pp. A1, A2.

8. Etherton, S. (2002). *Let's talk patents*. Tempe, AZ: Rocket Science Press.

Using a Patent

1. Allen, K. (2003). *Bringing new technology to market*. Upper Saddle River, NJ: Prentice Hall.

2. Rivette, K., & Kline, D. (2000, January–February). Discovering new value in intellectual property. *Harvard Business Review*, 2–10.

3. Etherton, S. (2002). *Let's talk patents*. Tempe, AZ: Rocket Science Press.

4. Etherton, S. (2002). *Let's talk patents*. Tempe, AZ: Rocket Science Press.

5. Allen, K. (2003). *Bringing new technology to market*. Upper Saddle River, NJ: Prentice Hall.

6. Jaffe, A., & Lerner, J. (2004). *Innovation and our discontents*. Princeton, NJ: Princeton University Press.

7. Silverman, A. (2002). I'll see you in court—Overview of a patent infringement trial. *JOM, 54*(5), 64.

8. Etherton, S. (2002). *Let's talk patents*. Tempe, AZ: Rocket Science Press.

9. Gomes, L. (2005, March 30). eBay wins fresh legal victory in challenge involving patents. *Wall Street Journal*, p. A6.

10. Greenhouse, L. (2007, January 10). Justices alter patent landscape. *The Plain Dealer*, p. C2.

11. Jaffe, A., & Lerner, J. (2004). *Innovation and its discontents*. Princeton, NJ: Princeton University Press.

12. Kaminski, M. (2006). Effective management of U.S. patent litigation. *Intellectual Property and Technology Law Journal, 18*(1), 13–25.

13. Heinzel, M. (2005, March 17). Blackberry maker agrees to settle patent dispute. *Wall Street Journal*, pp. B5, B5.

14. Bulkeley, W. (2005, March 2). Patent ruling irks inventors, aids companies. *Wall Street Journal*, pp. B1, B2.

15. Allen, K. (2003). *Bringing new technology to market*. Upper Saddle River, NJ: Prentice Hall.

16. Montgomery, C. (2004, July 20). Drive-in dry-dock. *The Plain Dealer*, pp. C1, C6.

17. Paris, E. (1999, November). David v. Goliath. *Entrepreneur*. Retrieved from http://www.entrepreneur.com/magazine/entrepreneur/1999/november/18480.html

18. Varchaver, N. (2006, July 10). Who's afraid of Nathan Myhrvold? *Fortune*. Retrieved from http://money.cnn.com/magazines/fortune/fortune_archive/2006/07/10/8380798/index.htm

19. Levy, S. (2006, March 13). The Blackberry deal is patently absurd. *Newsweek*. Retrieved from http://www.msnbc.msn.com/id/11677343/site/newsweek

Should You Patent?

1. Jaffe, A., & Lerner, J. (2004). *Innovation and its discontents*. Princeton, NJ: Princeton University Press.

2. Jaffe, A., & Lerner, J. (2004). *Innovation and its discontents*. Princeton, NJ: Princeton University Press.

3. Etherton, S. (2002). *Let's talk patents*. Tempe, AZ: Rocket Science Press.

4. Chesbrough, H. (2001). The patent and licensing exchange: Enabling a global IP marketplace. *Harvard Business School Teaching Note*, No. 5-601-124.

5. Reitzig, M. (2004). Strategic management of intellectual property. *Sloan Management Review, 45*(3), 35–40.

6. Jaffe, A., & Lerner, J. (2004). *Innovation and its discontents*. Princeton, NJ: Princeton University Press.

7. Etherton, S. (2002). *Let's talk patents*. Tempe, AZ: Rocket Science Press.

8. Richmond, R. (2005, May 4). Symantec patent may disturb rivals. *Wall Street Journal*, p. B3a.

9. Jaffe, A., & Lerner, J. (2004). *Innovation and its discontents*. Princeton, NJ: Princeton University Press.

10. Etherton, S. (2002). *Let's talk patents*. Tempe, AZ: Rocket Science Press.

11. Levin, R., Klevorick, A., Nelson, R., & Winter, S. (1987). Appropriating the returns from industrial research and development. *Brookings Papers on Economic Activity, 3*, 783–832.

12. Miller, S. (1996). Should patenting of surgical procedures and other medical techniques be banned? *IDEA: The Journal of Law and Technology*, 255–273.

13. Levin, R., Klevorick, A., Nelson, R., & Winter, S. (1987). Appropriating the returns from industrial research and development. *Brookings Papers on Economic Activity, 3*, 783–832.

14. Levin, R., Klevorick, A., Nelson, R., & Winter, S. (1987). Appropriating the returns from industrial research and development. *Brookings Papers on Economic Activity, 3*, 783–832.

15. Mullins, J. (2003). *The new business road test*. London: Financial Times, Prentice Hall

Secrecy

1. Afuah, A. (2003). *Innovation management*. New York: Oxford University Press.

2. Nelson, R., & Winter, S. (1982). *An evolutionary theory of economic change*. Cambridge, MA: Belknap Press.

3. Teece, D. (1998). Capturing value from knowledge assets: The new economy, markets for know-how and intangible assets. *California Management Review, 40*(3), 55–79.

4. Zucker, L., Darby, M., & Brewer, M. (1998). Intellectual human capital and the birth of U.S. biotechnology enterprises. *American Economic Review, 88*(1), 290–305.

5. Winter, S. (2000). Appropriating the gains from innovation. In G. Day & P. Schoemaker (Eds.), *Wharton on managing emerging technologies*. New York: John Wiley.

6. Teece, D. (1998). Capturing value from knowledge assets: The new economy, markets for know-how and intangible assets. *California Management Review, 40*(3), 55–79.

7. Chally, J. (2004). The law of trade secrets: Toward a more efficient approach. *Vanderbilt Law Review, 57*(4), 1269–1311.

8. Yoffie, D. (2003). Intellectual property and strategy. *Harvard Business School Note*, No. 9-704-493.

9. Chally, J. (2004). The law of trade secrets: Toward a more efficient approach. *Vanderbilt Law Review, 57*(4), 1269–1311.

10. Schilling, N. (2005). *Strategic management of technological innovation*. New York: McGraw-Hill.

11. Chally, J. (2004). The law of trade secrets: Toward a more efficient approach. *Vanderbilt Law Review, 57*(4), 1269–1311.

12. Allen, K. (2003). *Bringing new technology to market*. Upper Saddle River, NJ: Prentice Hall.

13. Fitzpatrick, W., DiLullo, S., & Burke, D. (2004). Trade secret piracy and protection: Corporate espionage, corporate security and the law. *Advances in Competitiveness Research, 12*(1): 57–68.

14. Schreiner, B. (2005, July 24). Colonel's recipe remains a secret. *The Columbus Dispatch*, pp. G1, G2.

15. Wingfield, N. (2006, June 28). At Apple, secrecy complicates life but maintains buzz. *Wall Street Journal*, pp. A1, A11.

16. Allen, K. (2003). *Bringing new technology to market*. Upper Saddle River, NJ: Prentice Hall.

17. Pettypiece, S. (2004). Biomec alleges that ex-manager gaves secrets to rival. *Crain's Cleveland Business*. Retrieved from http://www.crainscleveland.com/article/20041004/SUB/410040741&SearchID=73332238145390

18. Karush, S. (2005, March 23). IBM settles suit over intellectual property. *The Plain Dealer*, p. B2.

19. Guth, R. (2005, July 20). Microsoft sues to keep aide from Google. *Wall Street Journal*, pp. B1, B3.

20. Farkas, K. (2004, August 31). Patio enclosures awarded $8.6 million in suit. *The Plain Dealer*, p. D1.

21. Woolf, L. (2004, Summer). Non-competition agreements. *FDCC Quarterly*, 333–342.

22. Guth, R. (2005, July 20). Microsoft sues to keep aide from Google. *Wall Street Journal*, pp. B1, B3.

23. Woolf, L. (2004, Summer). Non-competition agreements. *FDCC Quarterly*, 333–342.

24. Hart, M. (1996). Palm Computing Inc. (A). *Harvard Business School Case*, No. 9-396-245.

Copyrights

1. Silverman, A. (1997). Understanding copyrights: Ownership, infringement, and fair use. *JOM, 49*(8), 60.

2. U.S. Department of Commerce. (1992). *General information concerning copyrights*. Washington, DC: U.S. Government Printing Office.

3. Austen, I. (2005, May 20). Block by block toy competitors build a case against Lego. *The Plain Dealer*, pp. G1, G5.

4. Mesa, P., & Burgelman, R. (2004). Finding the balance: Intellectual property in the digital age. In G. Burgelman, C. Christiansen, and S. Wheelwright (Eds.), *Strategic management of technology and innovation* (pp. 398-409). New York: McGraw-Hill Irwin.

5. U.S. Department of Commerce. (1992). *General information concerning copyrights*. Washington, DC: U.S. Government Printing Office.

6. Silverman, A. (1997). Understanding copyrights: Ownership, infringement, and fair use. *JOM, 49*(8), 60.

7. U.S. Department of Commerce. (1992). *General information concerning copyrights*. Washington, DC: U.S. Government Printing Office.

8. McBride, S. (2006, May 17). Music industry sues XM over replay device. *Wall Street Journal*, B1, B10.

9. Kiron, D. (2001). Napster. *Harvard Business School Case*, No. 9-801-219.

10. Moon, Y. (2005). Online music distribution in a post-Napster world. *Harvard Business School Case*, No. 9-502-093.

11. Silverman, A. (1997). Understanding copyrights: Ownership, infringement, and fair use. *JOM, 49*(8), 60.

12. Yoffie, D. (2003). Intellectual property and strategy. *Harvard Business School Note*, No. 9-704-493.

13. Moon, Y. (2005). Online music distribution in a post-Napster world. *Harvard Business School Case*, No. 9-502-093.

14. Associated Press. (2007, January 31). Sony BMG to reimburse customers for CD damage. *Wall Street Journal*, p. B4.

15. Smith, B., & Mann, S. (2004). Innovation and intellectual property protection in the software industry: An emerging role for patents. *University of Chicago Law Review, 71*, 241–264.

16. Barnett, W., & Leslie, M. (2006). Facebook. *Stanford Graduate School of Business Case*, No. E-220.

17. Yoffie, D. (2003). Intellectual property and strategy. *Harvard Business School Note*, No. 9-704-493.

18. Silverman, A. (1997). Understanding copyrights: Ownership, infringement, and fair use. *JOM, 49*(8), 60.

19. Smith, B., & Mann, S. (2004). Innovation and intellectual property protection in the software industry: An emerging role for patents. *University of Chicago Law Review, 71*, 241–264.

Trademarks

1. Silverman, A. (2005). How to customize and maximize federal trademark protection. *JOM, 57*(10), 72.

2. Clark, D. (2007, January 12). At the heart of Cisco's iPhone lawsuit: A desire for open standards. *Wall Street Journal*, p. A9.

3. Gleick, J. (2004, March 21). Get out of my namespace. *New York Times Magazine*, 44–49.

4. Gleick, J. (2004, March 21). Get out of my namespace. *New York Times Magazine*, 44–49.

5. U.S. Department of Commerce. (1992). *General information concerning trademarks*. Washington, DC: U.S. Government Printing Office.

6. Silverman, A. (2005). How to customize and maximize federal trademark protection. *JOM, 57*(10), 72.

7. Schilling, M. (2005). *Strategic management of technological innovation*. New York: McGraw-Hill.

8. Etherton, S. (2002). *Let's talk patents*. Tempe, AZ: Rocket Science Press.

9. Clark, D. (2007, January 12). At the heart of Cisco's iPhone lawsuit: A desire for open standards. *Wall Street Journal*, p. A9.

10. Cohen, D. (1991). Trademark strategy revisited. *Journal of Marketing, 55,* 46–59.

11. Kopp, S., & Suter, T. (2000). Trademark strategies online: Implications for intellectual property protection. *Journal, 19*(1), 119–131.

12. Allen, K. (2003). *Bringing new technology to market.* Upper Saddle River, NJ: Prentice Hall.

13. Chan, S. (2005, June 5). You can take the A train, but don't take its logo: You may get a warning letter. *New York Times*, p. 27.

14. Flandez, R. (2006, November 28). Tiny firm wins "chewy Vuiton" suit, but feels bite. *Wall Street Journal,* pp. B1, B5.

15. Vermette, N. (2000). Domain names in the realm of trademark law. *FICC Quarterly, 51*(1), 1–15.

16. Vermette, N. (2000). Domain names in the realm of trademark law. *FICC Quarterly, 51*(1), 1–15.

17. Kopp, S., & Suter, T. (2000). Trademark strategies online: Implications for intellectual property protection. *Journal, 19*(1), 119–131.

18. Bagby, J., & Ruhnka, J. (2004). Protecting domain name assets. *The CPA Journal, 74*(4), 64–67.

19. Gleick, J. (2004, March 21). Get out of my namespace. *New York Times Magazine,* 44–49.

20. Bagby, J., & Ruhnka, J. (2004). Protecting domain name assets. *The CPA Journal, 74*(4), 64–67.

Index